Hoffnung's

LITTLE ONES

The drawings contained in this small volume have been selected from illustrations made by Hoffnung for a sequence of articles entitled *Points for Parents*. These were written by Lady Elizabeth Pakenham (now Lady Longford) in the early fifties. The series originally appeared in the feature columns of the 'Daily Express' and, shortly afterwards was published in book form. However much times have changed, Hoffnung's reflections on small children remain irresistibly relevant today.

Books in print by
GERARD HOFFNUNG

Hoffnung's The Maestro
The Hoffnung Symphony Orchestra
The Hoffnung Music Festival
The Hoffnung Companion to Music
Hoffnung's Musical Chairs
Hoffnung's Acoustics
Hoffnung's Little Ones

Hoffnung's

LITTLE ONES

The Hoffnung Partnership

LONDON 2001

First published 1954
in book format as
Points for Parents
by Weidenfeld & Nicolson

Second publication 1961
Hoffnung's Little Ones
by Dennis Dobson

Third publication 1988
by Souvenir Press

This edition published 2001
by The Hoffnung Partnership
44 Pilgrims Lane
London NW3 1SN

ISBN 1-903643-05-8

Cover and book design
Vera Brice and Leslie Robinson

Printed and bound in Great Britain by
St Edmundsbury Press
Blenheim Industrial Park, Newmarket Road
Bury St Edmunds, Suffolk IP33 3TU

Acknowledgements

*Grateful thanks are due to Roger McGough
for his contribution to this book; and also to its designers
and printers for the infinite care and consideration
they have taken in its production.*

FOREWORD

What a joyous talent was Gerard Hoffnung!
Yours sincerely,
Roger McGoughnung

Am I like
papa.....

... or Mama...

...or Uncle
Horatio.....

.... or Great-
Aunt Phoebe.

Or ...

... am ...   ... I ...   ... like ...

...some... ....body... ..else.

Or am I

like me?

A Recital (continuoso).

There, there, there .....(etc.)

A complete Mystery.

Mistakes
are liable to
be made.

Hoffnung

" Matilda told such dreadful lies,
it made one gasp and stretch one's eyes."

Goodnight !

Hoffnung's The Maestro
Foreword by Sir Simon Rattle ISBN 1 903643 00 7

The Hoffnung Symphony Orchestra
Foreword by Sir Peter Ustinov ISBN 1 903643 01 5

The Hoffnung Music Festival
Foreword by Ronald Searle ISBN 1 903643 02 3

The Hoffnung Companion to Music
Foreword by Harry Enfield ISBN 1 903643 03 1

Hoffnung's Musical Chairs
Foreword by Ian Hislop ISBN 1 903643 04 X

Hoffnung's Acoustics
Foreword by Emily Hoffnung ISBN 1 903643 05 8